T0158818

POETRY
FROM THE
HEART

Mary Wilcox Young

authorHOUSE®

AuthorHouse™
1663 Liberty Drive
Bloomington, IN 47403
www.authorhouse.com
Phone: 833-262-8899

© 2021 Mary Wilcox Young. All rights reserved.

No part of this book may be reproduced, stored in a retrieval system, or transmitted by any means without the written permission of the author.

Published by AuthorHouse 07/22/2021

ISBN: 978-1-6655-3071-2 (sc)
ISBN: 978-1-6655-3070-5 (e)

Print information available on the last page.

Any people depicted in stock imagery provided by Getty Images are models, and such images are being used for illustrative purposes only.
Certain stock imagery © Getty Images.

This book is printed on acid-free paper.

Because of the dynamic nature of the Internet, any web addresses or links contained in this book may have changed since publication and may no longer be valid. The views expressed in this work are solely those of the author and do not necessarily reflect the views of the publisher, and the publisher hereby disclaims any responsibility for them.

CONTENTS

I Am Who I Am 1

A Fighter 2

A Man 3

A Praying Mother 4

A Strong Woman 5

An Anointed Vessel 6

Being Afflicted 7

Break Through 8

Breaking Up 9

Christmas 10

Church Folks 11

Don't Add to God Word 12

Don't Be Messy 13

Don't Get Weary 14

Honoring those Who Paved the Way 15

Easter 16

Education 17

Family 18

Flawless Vessel 19

Get Your Time In 20

God Created HELL 21

God Is 22

Going to God House 23

He Say She Say 24

Hear My Cry 25

Heaven 26

Hold Fast to God Word 27

Honoring Our Pastor 28

I Am Have Overcome 29

I'm A Soldier 30

It Was My Time 31

Just One Visit 32

Mothers...33

Praise Ye the Lord 34

Pray Without Ceasing...35

Prayer Is 36

Prophecy 37

Relationship 38

Repent 39

Run and Don't Look Back 40

Stress 41

Sweethearts Day.. 42

The Devil Is A Deceiver... 43

The Doctor 44

Thinking Out Loud.. 45

Use Your Gift 46

Wake Up 47

What is a S P E L L 48

When God Say Go..49

When Sick and Shut - In.. 50

Who is Satan?..51

He Picked Me 52

Women on the Battlefield...53

You Can Run, But You Can't Hide 54

I AM WHO I AM

When death comes it hard to take
We feel in our mind it's a big mistake
I didn't say bye, it's just not me
I'll say, see you later, that's what you always heard from me
I AM WHO I AM: who can you blame
I enjoyed my life, I wasn't ashamed.
Last week we were celebrating my brother birthday,
He didn't know he would be doing my eulogy, here today.
If you are holding hate down in your heart,
Pray let it go, turn it over to GOD.
I know you came to see me laid to rest,
I'm in the hands of the one who love me the best.
I don't need no car, don't need to ride the bus,
Nor do I need you to stay behind and argue and fuss.
Don't play, play, you may not live to see another day.
Talk with you month and not with your hands,
You don't have to provide you're the badder man.
I ain't going out with the low-low,
The LORD don't let me suffer, that one thing for sure.
Help not hurt, I do mean, let it come from your heart,
Don't do it to be seen. Enough is enough.
That's what you better say, the devil thought he had me
I went giving GOD praise.
You have your story about my life, GOD got the truth,
It's been recorded down, and yours have too.
I'm gone now, you just looked on me,
I'm no longer bound; I've been made free.
No more heartache, no more pain.
Disappointment had to go, the moment the LORD stood in the door.
You watched me, now I'm watching you.
He's coming back again, and that's the truth.
Hold it in the road, the ones I'm walking on been paved with gold. AMEN

IN LOVING MEMORIES OF KATHY DENISE WILCOX

A FIGHTER

A Fighter, **A Warrior**, whom you may know.
Invading the **Devil Territory**, don't care who shows,
Putting up their dukes, with their boxing gloves on.
Engaging in battle; telling the **Devil** to bring it on.
Using their weapon, the "**WORD**" which is a **two-edged sword,**
Bullying the **Devil,** not giving him a head start.
Calling out "**SPIRIT**", making them mad.
Walking in the **ANOINTING**, something the **Devil** once had.
Single combat, not standing along,
Carrying out orders that been handed down from "**GOD's**" **THRONE**.
Like a **Colorful Butterfly**; a **Sting in a Bee**,
The enemy want take **money**, to step in the ring with **thee**.
Head Strong; to stubborn to take down.
Standing Up; you can't shut them up.
If **Sitting Down**; they'll still **Thrown Down**.
A Pilot with Force; on the move; you don't get out of their way,
They'll make a **Runway** out of you.
A person with the **will**; the courage to carry it out,
A **determination** they have; and the **ability to stay in the fight**.

A MAN

A **Woman:** Wants a man who has a plan,
Who she can be proud to call her man?
A **Man:** That stands on his own,
Not afraid to leave home.
A **Man:** With a job, who honor **"GOD"**.
A **Man:** With a dream, who will treat her as his queen,
Not seeing other women in between.
A **Man:** She can touch, and feel, not complaining about bills.
A **Man:** Who's not afraid to say no, to female's he know.
A **Man:** She can trust, not one who like to argue, and fuss.
A **Man:** Of strength, and power, who she can rely on any given hour.
A **Man:** Of faith, who will deny his ways, and give **"GOD"** praise.
A **Man:** That finds a wife, finds a good thing.
Let your journey begin, keep **"JESUS"** in and they want win.

A PRAYING MOTHER

A **Praying Mother;** Stands her ground,
Sending up **prayers** reaching **"GOD Throne".**
Not being tossed, by every wind that blows her way,
Listening to the **"LORD"** and **Obeying** what **HE** says.
Praying for her **family,** and **friends,**
Asking the **"LORD",** to guide them in,
She knows the value of **"Prayer",**
Always looking to the hill's which cometh her help.
"Prayer", brings in change, kicking against a **praying.**
Mother is a dangerous thing.
They speak up and plead your case, asking,
The **"LORD"** to guide you as you run this race.
A **Praying Mother:** Want give up, she keeps **praying,**
For those who she knows has **slipped up.**
An **intercessor:** is who she has become, her life
Belong to the **"LORD"** until **HE** carry her home.
Not knowing what to **pray** for from Day to Day,
But the **spirit intercedes** and has its own way.
A **Praying Mother:** Don't **pray** in **doubt!**
She has **confidence** in **"GOD"** knowing **HE'LL** bring her out.
Be **encourage Mother's;** keep standing your **ground,**
When this **battle is over,** you will receive your **Crown.**
Keep the **"Faith",** go **boldly** before the **"Throne of Grace".**
Always give thanks for his Mercy and Grace.

A STRONG WOMAN

A woman of strength with a smile on her face,
Whom set and atmosphere of praise in any place.
Strong, watchful, free as can be,
Who allow patience, to have her perfect work in thee?
A fighter, a warrior, whom people have a privilege to know,
Invading the **Devil Territory** whenever he shows.
A woman with a will; the courage to carry it out,
A determination she has, and the ability to stay in the fight.
A STRONG WOMAN: Too hard to brake, founded on a solid!
Foundation, that the devil himself, find it hard to shake.
A STRONG WOMAN: The Lord catch the tears as they roll
Down her face, filling her with love as she run this race.
A STRONG WOMAN: No **shucking** and **jiving,**
A passenger in the seat **"JESUS"** doing the driving.
Many hard trails may come her way,
She has endurance because of her "**Faith**".
A **strong backbone**; for other to lean on,
Who follows her dreams and let noting come in between.

AN ANOINTED VESSEL

"**Prophets**" were "**Anointed**" as well as the "**Priests**"
The "**Anointing**" they received came from our "**King**".
Cleansed by "**GOD**"; whose Glory want depart,
As long as **sin** don't **darken** their **heart.**
To be filled and to be poured out,
The "**Anointing**" is **power** to bring the **captured** out.
The "**Anointing**" is design to open your mind,
Not just to fall on you from time to time.
An "**Anointing**" Vessel teaches you, they also
Imparts "**Spiritual Gifts**"; into you.
Guide you through the **Spirit** because they hear it.
Not **hitting** and **missing** because there not **listening**.
An "**Anointing**" Vessel will always say!
You'll the one who brought "**GOD**" this way.

BEING AFFLICTED

BEING AFFLICTED; is not all bad.
Take a look at **JOB**!
He was smitten with all **He** had.
Set up by **"GOD"**, "who knew his **Heart**.
JOB: love it couldn't **depart**.
BEING AFFLICTED; in distress **"JESUS CHRIST"**,
He had to embrace, no comfort, suffering he endured.
Complete confidence in his father who sent him to do it.
BEING AFFLICTED; depression is on the rise, sadness
Down **heartiness, murdering** taking place,
Right before our very eyes.
BEING AFFLICTED; can cause so much pain!
Stay focus, some things there is no one to blame.
Call on **Him; He's** on his **Way**,
He's holding back **destruction;** we better "**Pray**".
Amen

BREAK THROUGH

Hurricane "**JESUS**" is coming through!
He'll shake you up, and you will break through.
Like a tornado **HE** will spin you around,
When you acknowledge **Him**, **HE** will show up and throw down.
Push give birth, release that man child throughout this earth.
Break Through come on out; let this be your turning point.
Walk out, don't look back.
*Give the devil a **broke back**.*
*A **Black Eye** is what he needs.*
Give it to him by sowing seeds.
Pull his *teeth*, one by one, we can do it through **GOD SON!**
We are troubled on every side, yet not distressed
We are protective by a **SAVIOR,** who knows us best
We are perplexed, but not in despair.
When sickness shows up, the stripes of "**JESUS**" is right there.
Turn, run free yourself send up **Praises** in the atmosphere.
For the *ruler of this world* is coming,
The "**ANOINTING of GOD**" will keep him running!
Throw them *darts*, let them go through his *heart*.
Watch him bleed "**JESUS**" want to *intercede*.
Send him *packing*, while he's *attacking*.
You will have **enemies** everywhere you go,
Fill up with "**GOD WORD**" your give him a *hard blow*.

BREAKING UP

BREAKING UP is hard to do, when you really love someone.
You'll miss the talks and remember the long walks.
The hugs, and kisses, the meals, you shared cooking in the kitchen.
Breakfast in bed all the fun you had.
The movies shows you don't want to watch anymore.
That soft voice whispering in your ear, that you no longer hear.
The trips you took at vacation time, that you find,
Hard getting out of your mind.
The birthday cards that came from their heart,
That holiday fun, when you were Standing as one.
Them being your best friend, Who you thought you have to the end
Living in your home that were your own.
Grilling meat on the grill preparing their favorite meal.
The laughter you shared when no one else were there,
All the memories you had, is still there.
BREAKING UP is hard to do; give it to **JESUS**, He'll see you through.

CHRISTMAS

Christmas comes once a year,
Bringing families together far and near.
We should be celebrating the "BIRTH OF CHRIST"!
He already knows who's naughty or nice.
This is the day our SAVIOR was born,
We as the saints of "GOD" should be sounding the alarm.
Letting the world know "JESUS" is the reason,
For the season, we must strive to do what's pleasing.
He brought joy to the world,
Delight, happiness to every creature right here on earth.
"JESUS" was born in Bethlehem!
The wise men came to worship HIM,
Bringing gifts to the Newborn KING!
Myrrh, and Frankincense, as they entered in,
Honoring and adoring the "KING of KING"!
Let's celebrate the birth of "CHRIST"
Reminding everyone why he was crucified.

CHURCH FOLKS

Envy and jealousy are what they have in.
They have their eyes on you the moment you walk in.
Sitting back watching, trying to figure you out.
To come up with a plot to turn you back out.
Busy bodies are who they are.
Keep being that way, they won't go far.
Proud, boasters think they know everything.
Come to church every Sunday still haven't changed.
Murdering one another with that tongue in their mouth.
Get mad at the Pastor, because they want let them control God's house.
Draw nigh to God and he'll draw nigh to you.
Purify your hearts as the word instructs us to do.
Who try to change God word into a lie?
Nobody but them church folks think their sin is getting by.

DON'T ADD TO GOD WORD

DON'T ADD TO GOD WORD; nor take anything away,
There will be a **Judgment** we'll stand before one day.
"GOD" WORD is **true**, **HIS Commandment HE** order us to do.
Support **HIS WORD** stay committed,
Study everyday so **HE** can reveal the mystery within it.
Things **unexplainable,** will become **tangible.**
HIS secrets will be revealed, open up to those who are **HIS.**
Stay **Honest,** be **TRUE**; when the **Wrath** of **"GOD"** be poured out,
It want take its toll on you.
Don't add to **"GOD WORD",** it's tight but right!
His Apostle followed orders, they couldn't afford
To turn back.
They shared their testimony; each one had their own.
The work they were appointed to do, they couldn't have
Done on their own.
They were chosen by **"GOD", He** knew their **HEART'S,**
They didn't add to **"GOD WORD",** nor let nothing tare them apart.
Plagues they knew, the **"LORD Himself"** would do,
Taking away from **"GOD WORD";** we must not do.

DON'T BE MESSY

DON'T BE MESSY, always starting things,
That's between **You** and the **Devil**,
"JESUS" is **Nowhere** in **Between**.
Broadcasting somebody **Business** all over the **Place**,
Get mad if they confront you **Face** to **Face**.
A **Busy Body** just can't set **Still**,
Ear Dropping on **someone** else **Business**!
Trying to find somebody to tell.
Gossiper, nothing but a **Talebearer**!
Always Rejoicing over another **Man Trouble**.
Throwing a Stone; Hiding your **Hand** behind your back,
WE REAP WHAT WE SOW, AND THAT'S A TRUE FACT!
Messy People Do Messy Things!
They think their "SINS" are being **Unseen**.
DON'T BE MESSY, it's not <u>YOU</u>; **Repent** to the "LORD"
TELL THE TRUTH!

DON'T GET WEARY

Don't get tired and worn-out,
Seek the "**LORD**" and ride your trials on out.
Be not weary in well doing'
The "**LORD**" is in control, and HE know what HE's doing.
The devil must obey, HIS every command'
Don't be ready to drop, leave it in the "**LORD**" hand.
You may be tired and sometime feel bushed'
That's the time the "**SPIRIT**" will give you a push.
Being disgusted want help at all,
That's what the enemy want, to see us all fall.
The enemy want to do us in'
HE knows if we have complete confidence in the "**LORD**",
HE can't win. Drained, exhausted is what weariness will do,
If you allow that spirit to overthrow you.
Neither be weary of the "**LORD**" correction'
Walking in obedience; will always bring in your blessing.
The "LORD" shall renew our strength!
We shall run, and not be weary, and walk, and not faint.
This is the "**WORD of GOD**", it's always on time not a moment too late.

HONORING THOSE WHO PAVED THE WAY

HONORING THOSE WHO PAVED THE WAY!
Who taught us to shut in with, **"JESUS"**?
Fast and pray!
Going on **Dedication** year after year,
Letting us know time is drawing near.
Gave us instructions on how to **Fast!**
Feeding our **SPIRIT** with food, so we can remain Steadfast.
Studying **His WORD,** so we will know **His Voice,**
Assembling ourselves together; in **Him** we **Rejoice.**
ANOINTING us down as we go down the **Prayer Line,**
Giving us a "**WORD**" one at a time.
Committed to the work of the "**LORD**" with their whole **Heart.**
Dedicated, **Praying** for their flock,
Encouraging us to pour out to the **LORD,** releasing all out.
Names Scandalize, people told **Lies,**
They stood in the gap, commanded death to get back.
Denied by family, who didn't know "**GOD**".
They had to keep pressing, with a hurtful **Heart.**
HONOR THOSE WHO PAVED THE WAY!
You will receive your **Reward,**
When you see "**JESUS**", **Face** to **Face.**

EASTER

EASTER SUNDAY is about the RESURRECTION OF "JESUS CHRIST"!
A Man who came and gave HIS LIFE.
BEING DISHONORED with DISGRACE, as they SPIT, in his FACE,
Because they were BOUND in their WICKED Ways.
Bruised DISCOLORED, Skin became BLACK,
Not one time did "HE" MUMBLED a word back.
Crown with THORNS, stuck through HIS HEAD,
ALL OF HIS ACCUSERS; just wanted HIM DEAD.
SPIKES DRIVEN THROUGH HIS HANDS,
HE was BRUTALLY BEATEN and could Hardly Stand.
For every NATION who except "HIM" in,
They took a SPEAR and ran it through HIS Side,
Stood there and watched as the BLOOD and WATER poured out.
A MAN WHO CARRIED HIS OWN CROSS,
BARED ALL OUR SINS, AS THEY "CRUCIFIED HIM" ON "THE CROSS".
AMEN

EDUCATION

Children, please get an **EDUCATION!**
This is very important for you, all through out your life,
Your EDUCATION will follow you through.
Before you enter the building say a **PRAYER** or two,
Asking the "LORD" for understanding, and guidance,
He will see you through.
If you have any questions, don't be afraid to raise your hand.
Others will hear the answers, and they may join on in.
Listen and respect your teachers, don't do what you see others do,
They are there to teach you, some give extra help too!
School is for your learning; it's not vacation time,
The Board of **EDUCATION** is working hard, so no child is left behind.

FAMILY

Are every family close knitted?
Or do we fill some are misfitted?
Family: is supposed to stick together,
Not low rate, and tear down each other.
FAMILY: Could become worn, or torn apart,
Especially those out of the will of **"GOD"**.
They can become broken, and filled with fear,
Grieving of their loved ones, who's no longer here.
FAMILY: Members can be straight forward, and right to the point,
While felling in our heart they don't have to be so blunt.
You can give advice, but some want listen.
They feel your old fashion and very superstitious.
FAMILY: And friends should keep their business within.
Praying families, stands together, bearing one another's burdens.
Would you pick them up if they lied on you or?
Would you run and hide because they have lie?
FAMILY: Will smile in your face, and chew on a bone, behind your back.
Don't be messy put the enemy to a flight.
And because iniquity shall abound, the love of many,
Shall wax cold, don't stand by and watch your family fold.
Fasting and praying, brings about change.
Destroying Families is what the devil hope to gain.
Put up a fight; Do what's right, Stay in **"GOD"** Plan,
Don't, Hearken to man.
"GOD" is faithful, He Is true!
Every individual stand before **"GOD"**,
For themselves, that means you.
Stay Meek Pray for the Weak.

FLAWLESS VESSEL

This is a poem the Lord had me to write down.
A flawless vessel can one be found?
I'm soon to appear will you be there?
I'm coming for my bride who has nothing to hide.
You can fake it, but you won't make it.
You can pretend but you will lose in the end.
Eternal is a life without an end.
That's the reward for those who are born again.
I'm flawless and I stand my ground.
My solid foundation can't be torn down.
Can't be ripped, split nor pulled apart.
I know my work, how can yours be so hard?
Faith moves me unconditional love I have for you.
My affection without limitations.
Love you receive not from being on bending knees.
Flawless without shame, can you look at your life and say the same.
Unblemished, unmarked allow my word to penetrate your heart.
No sins I have within, this is from the beginning to the end.
The horn of salvation, I offered myself to redeem all nations.
Listen to my speech, take heed to my voice.
I told you in my word I am a jealous God.

GET YOUR TIME IN

"JESUS" is coming; and it want be long.
We're going to have a **Feast** around **"GOD THRONE"**.
Praise Him now while you have time,
Be ye **Transformed**, by the **Renewing** of your **MIND**.
Don't copy the **Behavior,** and **Customs** of this **World**.
John; saw "**New Jerusalem**" coming down from **Heaven Above**.
GET YOUR TIME IN; open up let **Him** in.
He is "**Alpha, and Omega**"! the **Beginning** and the **End**.
Faithful, Holy, the only one who can forgive our **Sins**.
The **FIRST,** and the **LAST**, who don't **Discriminate** against your past.
The day of the "**LORD**" so cometh as a thief in the night.
Whom has given us much time to make things, right?

GOD CREATED HELL

Hell, a lake of fire, a bottomless pit.
Satan's Kingdom, "God is the creator of it.
The underworld, the shades below don't except.
CHRIST in "To Hell lost souls will go".
One another burdens can't no one bear.
Torment and suffering will be there.
A home of lost souls with grief and remorse.
All because they choose evil and wouldn't harken to God's voice.
The Abyss full of misery, despair and everlasting fire.
With Brimstone, flames everywhere.
Once they are in, they can't come out.
That's one main point the devil don't talk about.
Jesus spoke of outer darkness and a furnace of fire.
Where there will be wailing, weeping and gnashing of teeth.
They chose to stay bound they refuse to be free.
An awful smell they can't tell no one about.
Jesus has the keys that's one place no one can break out.
They will be tormented day and night forever.
All whose names are not written in the Lamb book of Life.
Satan can't win, he's not born again.
Hell is his judgement he will receive at the end.
AMEN

GOD IS

GOD IS: The **Creator of Heaven and Earth.**
HE created every man, woman, boy, and girl!
GOD IS a spirit you see, you must have **Faith**, and **Believe**.
When you wake up in the morning time,
Know that it was Him who touched your mind.
HE allows us to see a brand-new day!
Waiting to hear us when we pray.
Need someone to talk to at any given time.
JESUS is always on the main line.
HE sees everything we do family, friends our enemies too!
Having trouble on your job, pour out to **GOD** don't take it to Heart.
GOD will be your best friend; you must open up and let Him in.
If you want to know who **GOD** is; study His **Word**, He will be revealed.

GOING TO GOD HOUSE

HE is a "**GREAT KING** "over the **Earth!**
HE can fill your Hunger, and Quince your Thirst.
A SPIRIT of Liberty; should be there,
As "**Praise and Worship**" fill the **A**ir.
A house of refuge, safe from danger!
Praising our "**SAVIOR**," singing songs like **ANGELS**.
Praying to "**JESUS**", He'll hear us all,
As we come together as they make **Altar Call**.
GOING TO GOD HOUSE
Is a wonderful thing!
Receiving a **WORD** from the **KING of KING**.
Love, and laughter should be shown,
As we represent our "**SAVIOR**" who sits on the throne.
Testifying about "**JESUS**" who gave **H**is Life for us all!
It's not **H**is will that any of us fall.
When the preacher is preaching the "**WORD OF GOD**"
Give ear to what it says, let it **P**enetrate your **Heart**.
This is the purpose for going to "**GOD House**",
To receive **HIS** Instructions and carry them out.

HE SAY SHE SAY

He say, she say will get you hurt.
Running your mouth exposing out dirt.
Some false some true either way it does not concern you.
He say she say has been added in.
That's what happens when others put their two cents in.
Stay clear stop believing everything you hear.
He say she say causes nothing but trouble.
Let's pull together stop hating on one another.
He say she say what did Jesus say.
Death and life are in the power of the tongue.
Know that you will be talked about until your life here is done.

HEAR MY CRY

HEAR MY CRY "LORD" as I pour out my **HEART** to you,
REMOVE the **WOUNDS, HURT**, and **GRIEF** too!
HEAR MY CRY on a daily base,
As I give thanks, for your **SAVING GRACE!**
HEAR MY CRY as I pray for my **SONS**,
Keeping them Lifted up until my work here is done.
HEAR MY CRY "LORD" as I continue to fast,
Feeding my **SPIRIT** with food that will last.
HEAR MY CRY "Lord" as I open-up to you,
Seeking your **FACE** until I get my spiritual break through.
HEAR MY CRY as I pray for others, I'm my **"BROTHER KEEPER",**
That's all that matters.
HEAR MY CRY "Lord" as I seek you for wisdom and knowledge
Can't understand your word, I know without it.
HEAR MY CRY and give me understanding when trials come,
I can keep on standing.
HEAR MY CRY as I **Pray** for my **Leaders**,
Giving thanks to you, for having **Great Teachers.**
HEAR MY CRY is the name of this **POEM**,
I have Victory in **"JESUS"**, my **Battle** is already **WON!**

HEAVEN

Have you ever wondered what HEAVEN is like?
There will be no more SLEEPEST NIGHTS!
The streets are Paved with Gold,
Everyone there has been made WHOLE!
You are free in every way,
All day long, giving GOD PRAISE!
They can't CROWN HIM until we get there,
From SIGNS and WONDERS time is DRAWING NEAR!
HEAVEN IS GOD's DWELLING PLACE!
One day we will see HIM, FACE to FACE!

IT WAS MY TIME

It was my time; I know it's hard to let go.
He whispered in an honorable voice,
I just couldn't say no.
I was that **Peace Lily, Pretty, Green, and White!**
One you can look upon **Morning, Noon and Night**.
He wanted to plant me beside the quiet stream,
A **Lily,** which could always be looked upon, so **Pretty and Green**.
So, I gave Him my hand, as we **journeyed** to the **promise land,**
Looking to see my loved ones, those who made it in.
With a "**Praise**" in my **heart**, and a **dance** in my **feet**,
Seeing our **SAVIOR**; whom we all want to **meet and greet**.
So much joy, and excitement; "**GOD's**" **GLORY** in the air,
The choir singing; angels rejoicing everywhere.
It was my time you see; **HE** chose me!
I've been made free, no more suffering,
To endure, "**ETERNAL LIFE**"; I received the moment,
I walked through the door.
Amen

JUST ONE VISIT

JUST ONE VISIT is all it takes,
To be shared with Someone,
You love and **appreciate**!
Someone who may have been left along,
Not able to get up and do things on their own.
A **H**ug or Smile you both share,
JUST ONE VISIT showing Someone you CARE.
To laugh, or talk things on their mind out,
To help **encourage** their **faith** and cast down all **doubt**.
Be that shoulder for Someone to **lean** on,
Never leave them standing along.
JUST ONE VISIT could help make Someone Day!
When in their present remember to **PRAY**.
JUST ONE VISIT could cause Someone life to change!
When one or two come together and call on **"JESUS NAME"**.
Amen.

MOTHERS

MOTHERS; are always **Special**, standing in a class by themselves,
"**GOD**" gave them such a love, to **Nurture**, and **Protect** someone **else.**
Mothers: always have a **Job** to do,
Cleaning, Cooking, and "**Praying**" you threw.
Visiting the **School, Doctor Appointments**, as well,
Giving you much, **Tender Loving Care.**
This can't be dropped in someone else lap.
Our minds become "**GOD**" Road map.
Always on the go, making stops from **store to store,**
Trying to find the best **deals**, making sure you get a **meal.**
Dealing with your **likes** and **dislikes.**
Praying to "**GOD**", we raise you right,
Paying bills and so much more, all you do is walk through the door.
Give thanks to "**GOD**" for **Mothers**; all around the **World**!
Most of all be Thankful to "**GOD**" for **Yours.**

PRAISE YE THE LORD

PRAISE YE THE LORD, with your whole HEART!
Only the PURE in HEART, shall see GOD.
For the works of the LORD are great,
HE's to wise and HE makes no mistakes.
"HOLY SPIRIT, HOLY GHOST" let your SPIRIT take control.
Praise the LORD, in the present of your enemies!
Let them see the joy the LORD put within you.
Praise the LORD, all ye nations: For HIS love, and HIS greatness.
O clap your hands, all ye "JESUS" fans,
Let the world know for righteousness, I stand.
Praise ye the LORD, HE's greatly to be praised,
Even in our trials we must praise HIM always.
For the WORD of the LORD is right, and praises is comely for the up right!
Let the people praise thee, O GOD: let all the people praise thee.
For in you we have the victory, our souls have been made free.
Praise ye the LORD, for the favor of our GOD.
Let everything that hath breath, praise the LORD
PRAISE YE THE LORD!

PRAY WITHOUT CEASING

PRAY WITHOUT CEASING: That mean nonstop.
Let us pour out to the **LORD** releasing all out.
Men should always pray; HE didn't tell us to bring it to an end.
PRAYING WITHOUT CEASING: Is a sure way to usher the **Spirit** in.
Prayer is in order, that how we communicate with our **SAVIOR.**
We don't know always what to Pray, for, but we know **GOD** it able.
It's Praying time; no time to pause!
The enemy is listening, he hears us as we call.
We can't refrain from Praying, we want stand.
The **LORD** Himself; is the one who give us patience within.
There's no time to cease, when we cease the enemy increase.
Don't quit, there's no time to stop; never allow the enemy,
To bring your prayer life to a halt.
Talk to the **LORD**, let your voice be heard.
Be persistent, hold fast, take **GOD** at His Word
The race is not given to the swift, nor the battle to the strong.
So, let's bow guard heaven, sending up prayers reaching **GOD Throne**.

PRAYER IS

PRAYER IS: the key,
Faith unlocks the door.
The more you **pray**,
"GOD" will open up to you **more, and more**.
PRAYER IS: Talking to "**GOD**",
Releasing honestly; what's in your heart.
Much prayer, much power!
You can talk to **HIM**, any given hour.
A **confident prayer life** is built,
On the **cornerstone** of "**CHRIST**".
PRAYER IS: Thanking "GOD"; for his Mercy and Grace!
PRAYER IS: Repenting on a daily base.
PRAYER will show you things about yourself,
The "**LORD**" order a good man step.
PRAYER IS: establishing a relationship with "GOD"!
One that the **devil** will try to **tear apart**.
PRAYER IS: Having "**GOD**" to talk to,
When **fear** and **doubt** set in on you.
PRAYER IS: Releasing all **guilt** and **shame!**
Knowing **Eternal Life**, you will gain.

PROPHECY

Prophecy is a gift that came forth from "**GOD**",
Don't get mad at the **Preacher**, if you fell to do your part.
He that has an ear to hear what the **SPIRIT** says,
You can't be trusted with any grift walking in your own way.
Prophecy is foretelling the future as well as the past,
If it's not according to **GOD's WORD** telling lies want last.
Prophecy is fore warning, sounding the alarm,
The enemy is seeking out whom he can cause harm.
We are pre-warned of the future and told about the past,
If the Lord never warn us as Saints, we wouldn't last.
Prophecy came not in by the will of man, but **Holy Men of "GOD"!**
As they are moved by the HOLY GHOST; they speak to people heart.
Whether there be **Prophecies**; they shall **Fail**.
Whether there be **Tongues**; they shall **Cease**.
Whether there be **knowledge**; it shall **vanish** away
But the "**WORD of GOD**"; It's here to stay.

RELATIONSHIP

When you're in a relationship that just not working.
Pack your bags and keep on trucking.
No matter what people laugh and do.
You know this is best for you.
Someone in the relationship may tear you down.
If not careful, your leave with hate not a frown.
How can two walk together except they agree.
If not with one accord, you'll be bound, and not free.
You can be in a relationship for years, and years.
Yet walk away with heartaches, and tears.
Whomsoever **GOD;** put together, let no man put Asunder.
Make sure your relationship is ordained by **GOD,**
If not, it can be torn apart.
Relationship when broken up, can cause you to leave,
With so much hurt, don't go straight into another one,
It just want work.

REPENT

REPENT for the **Kingdom** of **HEAVEN** is at hand!
We, one day, will leave this **PLACE,**
And cross over into a **New Land**!
There's no more **PEACE** for the **WICKED!**
They **REFUSE** to **Accept HIM** in.
REPENTANCE brings about a **CHANGE,**
A different **MINDSET** is what it **BRINGS.**
We should **REPENT,** daily **BASIS!**
Asking for **FORGIVENESS,** Thanking **HIM** for **HIS MERCY** and **GRACE.**
TRUE REPENTANCE is **a GODLY SORROW** for **SIN!**
Once you **POUR OUT; THE LORD** can **POUR IN.**
An act of **TURNING** around and going in the **OPPOSITE** direction,
HARKENING to **THE LORD,** following **HIS INSTRUCTION!**
CREATE in me a clean **HEART,** is what we are **ASKING** the **LORD,**
Unless you **REPENT,** "said **"JESUS",** you will all likewise **PERISH,**
In other Words; **WITHER AWAY; DECAY;** and be **DESTROYED!**
Because we wouldn't **REPENT!** and **EXCEPT, THE LORD** in our **HEART.**

RUN AND DON'T LOOK BACK

RUN AND DON'T LOOK BACK!
Never allow the enemy to cause you to back track.
Back tracking is backing up on **THE LORD!**
The relationship you shared,
The enemy have jealousy destroyed.
Don't take a glimpse back into your past,
HE's showing you things that **HE** knows want last.
It's nothing but a big slap right in your face,
Another trick **HE**'s throwing at you as you run this race.
Run, pick us up and put them down.
When the emps get in your path,
Run them over and knock them down.
Pray, commune with **THE LORD**; fall on bended knees.
There's no good thing **THE LORD** will withhold from thee.
HE knows our pass; **HE** separates us from **GOD**,
HE knows we want last.
Run and don't look back!
Give the enemy; the Devil all his partying tools back.

STRESS

Physical or Emotional tension, is what stress is,
Trust in "JESUS", I know HE heals!
A silence killer is what it will be,
If you allow your troubles to overwhelm thee.
Exercise, eat healthy is what the doctor says,
This is something we must practice, each day.
Stress can cause heart attack, strokes as well,
"Praying" for one another is something we can all share.
Being frustrated want help at all,
"JESUS", is there to hear us, all we must do is call.
Sleepless nights are what we will have,
If we allow stress to carry us there.
Look beside you, tell me what you see,
The ANGLE of "GOD", standing beside thee.
To lift the weight and make you free.
We're to BLESSED to be STRESS!
Stop allowing people to put you in their mess.
Turn it over to "JESUS"! He'll give you rest.
We'll serving a "MIGHTY GOD" who love us the best.

SWEETHEARTS DAY

SWEETHEART; My Baby My BOO!
Receive all this **Love**, only I can shower on **You**!
Stay in **Love**; don't let nothing cause you to go astray,
Express yourself in your own way every day.
Love conquers all, we keep holding each other,
We won't stumble and fall.
You are Mine, always on My Mind.
Smelling like a rose, very sweet,
Felling the tingles in my feet, as your heartbeat.
Standing there looking, with a smile on my face,
Cherishing each moment, we can embrace.
Hugging and Cuddling on this Special Day,
The Sweet Whisper in your Ear takes my breath away.
My Heart Pounding, Sounding so Loud,
Watch out Sweetie; you got my head in a cloud.
Sweet as Candy every Bite!
You're the only one, who can crave my Appetite.

THE DEVIL IS A DECEIVER

THE DEVIL IS A DECEIVER!
He tells many lies, making certain people don't understand,
THE REASON "JESUS" Died.
The "**WORD**" is being Preached going forth nationwide,
Tearing down strong Holds, especially that **SPIRIT** of Pride.
The Devil is a Slander, scared to stand along,
Sending out his go-getters; destroying happy homes.
He felled from "**GOD's**" favor, trying to take over his throne,
He got kicked right on out and didn't go along.
Nothing but a tempter he couldn't temp: **GOD!**
That's why he's angry trying to mimic **GOD.**
The wicked one is not going to stop; he's turning up the heat,
Trying to convince himself, that he cannot be beat.
His power is subject to **GOD's** restrictions, that's the way it is,
One thing he and his imps know, **JESUS CHRIST IS REAL!**

THE DOCTOR

A **Prayer,** a day keeps the **Doctor** Away!
Believe me when I say,
"**JESUS is LORD**", He'll do his part,
If you give it to Him from the start.
Doubt your doubt, give Him a Shout, in the mist of coming out,
Clap your hands, all you "**JESUS**" fans, let the world know,
He is the man; don't look down upon people for there's sins,
Through "**JESUS CHRIST**" you can be born again.
The Doctor is in the house, give your heart to him,
He can release the pain out.
Doctor, Lawyer, Constant Friend is he.
Thank you, "**JESUS**", for healing me.
Sickness is not always your body you see,
Your **love, joy, or peace** could have been stripped from thee.
Only "**JESUS**" can **restore,** and make you **free,**
All you must do is **believe**.

THINKING OUT LOUD

THINKING OUT LOUD: Is what we do,
When everything in life seen so gloomy!
THINKING OUT LOUD: Is what we do,
When we can't find a job and bills are due.
THINKING OUT LOUD: Is what we do,
When your hidden secrets eat away at you
THINKING OUT LOUD: is what we do,
When family and love ones turn their back on you.
THINKING OUT LOUD: is what we do,
When we don't have anyone to talk too.
THINKING OUT LOUD: is what we do,
When you're always helping others, and no one help you.
THINKING OUT LOUD: is what we do,
After raising Kids and they forget about you.
THINKING OUT LOUD: is what we do,
When we think about the task we're going through.
THINKING OUT LOUD: is what we do,
When **"JESUS"** has told us he's here to carry us through.
HE'LL never leave nor forsake you.

USE YOUR GIFT

USE your gift, do it with cheer, if you be a shame
Before man, that's a sure way your vision want stand.
Don't be timid, "**GOD**" isn't in it, rely on **HIM**,
HE'LL carry you through, HE gave you the gift, **HE'LL** complete it in you.
Stand firm you're not standing along, **HE'LL** turn every **SPIRIT**,
That tries to tare you down.
If HE gives you a song, sing it with joy!
"**THE ANOINTING of GOD**", the Devil can never **destroy**.
Use your feet, pick them up, put them down, send forth
A **praise** changes that atmosphere around.
*Use your **gift, stand bold** and **courageous**,*
Through **love** and **kindness**, you can reach all ages.
Your **gift** will make room for you,
Release it, help somebody else break through.
Your "**GOD**" given **gift** will cast out fear.
There is no stopper big enough to stop "**GOD**",
We all can do our part, let's pull together, mending broken **Hearts**.
HE hasn't given us a **gift,** to put on a shelf!
When we use it, we want loose it, but we must never abuse it.

WAKE UP

Wake up, with a "PRAYER" in your Mouth!
A Praise in your Heart, starting off your Day,
Giving Honor to our "God".
Wake up, arise from your Sleep, we've been Sleeping too long,
"JESUS" is about to come to carry the Saints; of "GOD" Home.
Wake up, sound the Alarm,
"JESUS" will send Peace, into every Broken Home.
Call on HIM, HE's on HIS way,
HE's sending forth Correction; Repent and Mend your Ways.
Wake up, time is Drawing Near,
Those who are Sound Asleep; will miss "Him" when "HE" APPEAR.
Wake up trouble is all Around!
If we Faint not, we shall Receive our Crown.
Trouble Don't Last Always, for the Elect Sake,
The "LORD" is Shortening our Days.
Wake up who's Voice you're going to Hear!
NO MAN KNOW THE DAY, NOR THE HOUR,
WHEN THE SON OF "MAN" SHALL APPEAR!

WHAT IS A SPELL

Is it evil, could it carry you to H E L L?
Is it wickedness going against GODLINESS?
Does it has the Power to Kill?
Or could it speak out be thy heald?
Could you pray a spell away?
Do you be a victim to what it say?
Is it a trick is it someone being cruel?
Just because they want control.
Could it hide and come to life?
Because of housing, envy, malice and strife.
Could it call you from the dead.
Or is it a hungry soul that was never fed?
Could jealousy play a part,
Because of hate you hold in your heart?
Or true love you don't want to depart.
What is a SPELL?
Do it come from witches who carry out your wishes?
Or A Wizard who love FAME,
Pulling you in the game because you have no Shame?
Is it something to quench your thirst,
Or would you say it's a generational curse?
When you're under a spell you been bewitched,
it's coming from someone who is digging a ditch.
They can't do the supernatural,
So, in their mind they're doing what come naturally.

WHEN GOD SAY GO

WHEN "GOD" SAY GO; put the **Pedal** to the **Floor!**
Where we stop only, "HE" knows, **WHEN "GOD" SAY GO,**
We have the ride away, give a deaf ear; to what **Critics** has to say.
Ride and let "JESUS" drive; no mistakes will be made "**HE's**" too **WISE**.
WHEN "GOD" SAY GO; hold on tight "JESUS" is our "MEDIATOR"
The **Enemy** himself has to **Step Back**!

WHEN SICK AND SHUT - IN

WHEN SICK AND SHUT- IN, sometimes we feel
Abandoned, even by our closest friend.
No one stops by, even to hear your heart cry.
Emotions on the rise, no one sees the tears, that flow from your eyes.
Feeling hopeless and despair; nothing else you care to bare.
Not able to get up and stir around,
Makes you feel like your while world is turned upside down.
Dwelling on your own sorrows, not wanting to face tomorrow.
Feeling helpless at all times,
The enemy trying to confuse your mind.
Many fears you constantly face, discouragement you can no longer embrace.
And the prayer of Faith shall save the sick, and the Lord shall raise him up.
Don't give up, "I will lift up mine eyes to the hills,
From whence cometh my help, even when you can't take a step.
WHEN SICK AND SHUT- IN; always remember
to allow the "**SPIRIT of GOD**" in!
Amen

WHO IS SATAN?

"**SATAN**", the ruler of this **World**; and the **Prince of the Power of the Air**!
You might not see him, but you know he's there.
The **Great Opposer, Adversary** of "**GOD**" and **Mankind,**
"**SATAN**" tries to blind people's understanding
as he plays tricks with their minds,
Not even caring it's just a waste of time.
"**SATAN**" the personal name of the **DEVIL**, you might want to add,
Every time we yield to him, he walk around glad.
The **DEVIL** is crazy, he don't have no **Sense**, he's running out of time,
So, he can't quit. **Destroying Families, Husbands, and Wives**
As well, confusing the mind, dragging **Souls** to **HELL**.
Deceiving young men, having them locked away in Jail,
Every time he succeed, he runs to his demons and tell.
HELL is enlarging herself **Daily**; that's what the **Bible** says, Unrepentant **SIN**,
NOT EXCEPTING "CHRIST" IN!
Can cause one to be on their way.

HE PICKED ME

I was that flower that had to be picked'
The LORD gave me time HE didn't make it quick!
Discharged from my duties here on earth,
Reliving my life, in heaven above.
I fought a good fight, I stayed on course,
I have made my entrance in heaven doors.
No more heart ache, no more pain,
Only eternal life, I have gained.
Everlasting life without end,
Hold onto the memories all my love ones, and friends.
Remember me as life goes on,
My book is closed, you must journey on.
To be absent from the body' is to be present with the LORD,
Life without me being here is heavy on your heart.
HE Picked Me, I'm Free, nothing by any means can hinder me.
Amen

WOMEN ON THE BATTLEFIELD

On this **Battlefield** be prepared to **Fight**!
Sitting out **Dynamite, Morning, Noon** and **Night**.
Follow orders don't always ask why,
Not being **Obedient** can cost you your **Life.**
Rules you must follow, **Discipline** you must have,
Undergoing training on someone else's behalf.
Study your "**WORD**", it's better than reading a map,
When trapped off on your journey, the "**HOLY GHOST**" will reveal it back.
Putting on the **Breastplate;** that **Bullet Proof Vest,**
As we enter the **Enemy Territory**,
Dropping Bombs, Blowing up his **Mess**.
Throw the **Grenade, don't be afraid,**
Watch him **burn**, he won't be able to **run**.
With a sword in your hand, representing for "**GOD**" I'm taking a stand.
There will be **Wounds**; there will be **Scars**!
This battle is not yours, it's the "**LORD's**".
Make the devil **surrender**, make him **quit**,
Make him leave the **Battlefield; bloody** and **wet**.
Stay **watchful, prayerful too, keep looking to the hills,**
The "**LORD**" **will carry you through**.
The **Victory** has already been **Won**!
"**THROUGH JESUS CHRIST, GOD SON**"!

YOU CAN RUN, BUT YOU CAN'T HIDE

YOU CAN RUN, BUT YOU CAN'T HIDE!
Jonah tried it, **He** almost died out of the belly of **Hell** he cried,
Three day and three nights.
Jonah **Prayed** unto the "**LORD**", trying to make things right.
He ran but he couldn't hide,
A sacrifice unto the Lord he made.
A voice of thanksgiving he gave,
The fish vomited Jonah out upon dry land.
Jonah took off "yes he knows "**GOD**" wasn't playing
You can run but you can't hide
From the presence of the **LORD** so don't even try it
Amen